Earning Allowance
with
Willow and Walter

Marcy Schaaf

In 2025, Willow and Walter had a brilliant idea: "Let's start earning an allowance!" They didn't let their wheelchairs slow them down—in fact, they saw chores as a fun way to help their family, earn some cash, and maybe even buy a treat or two.

From sweeping and mopping to feeding their furry friends, these two are ready to roll into action. Along the way, they'll discover that chores aren't just about money—they're about teamwork, responsibility, and having fun while helping everyone at home.

So grab your broom, your mop, and your biggest smile, and join Willow and Walter on their hilarious chore-filled adventure!

Willow and Walter, in chairs with wheels,
Plotted a plan with laughter and squeals.

Let's help out at home and
earn some dough!
We'll clean this house
from top to toe!

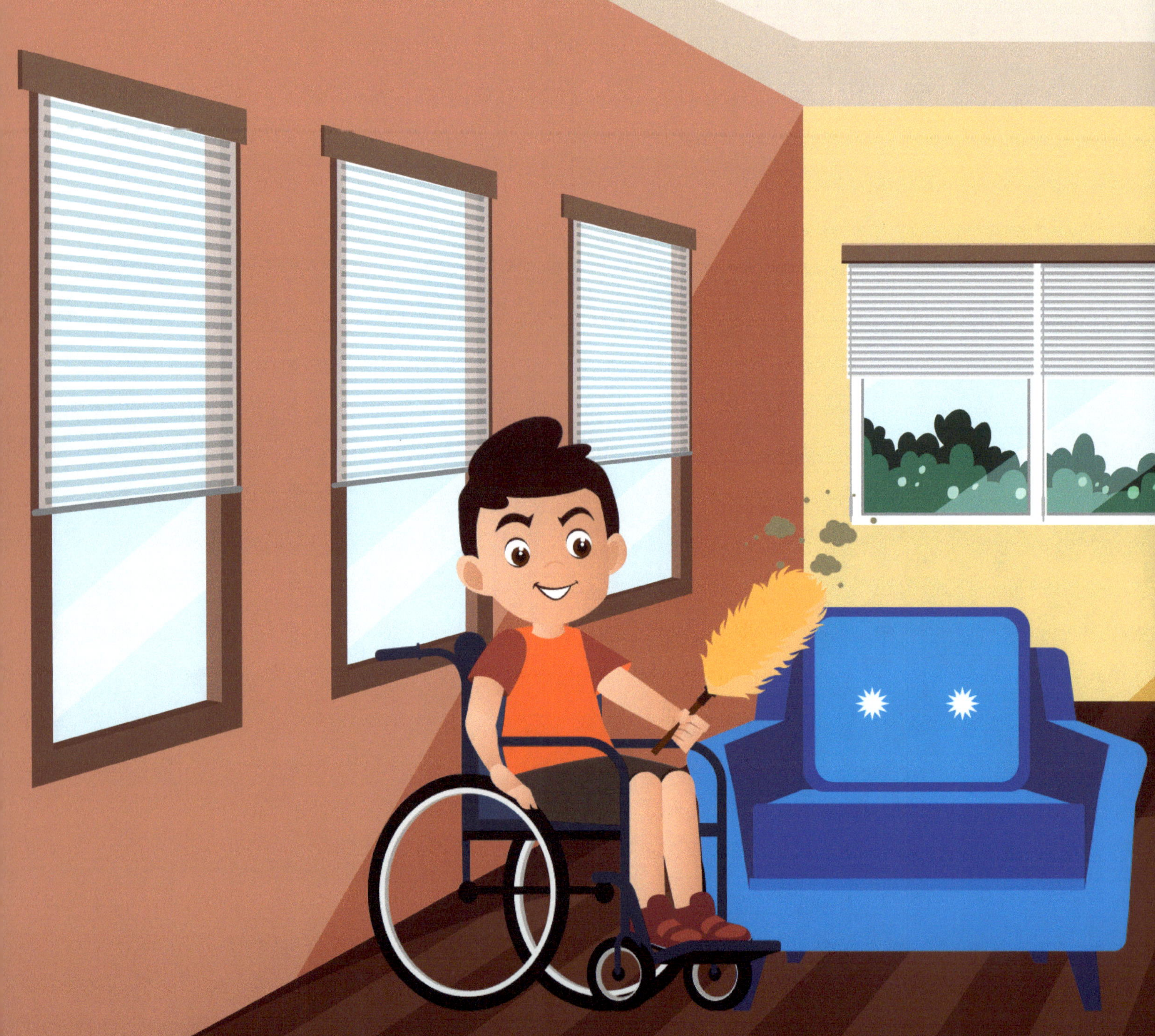

Willow dusted with a playful swat,
"Oops, I missed—
Walter, hold that!"

Walter grabbed the broom with a swooshy swish,
"I'll sweep the crumbs from last night's fish!"

Willow mopped with a zigzag twirl,
"I'll make this floor sparkle like a pearl!"

"Water the plants!" Walter gave a spin.
"Oops! Sorry, Willow, I splashed your chin!"

Rover barked
"Hey, don't forget me!"
Willow scooped kibble,
"Here's your spree!"

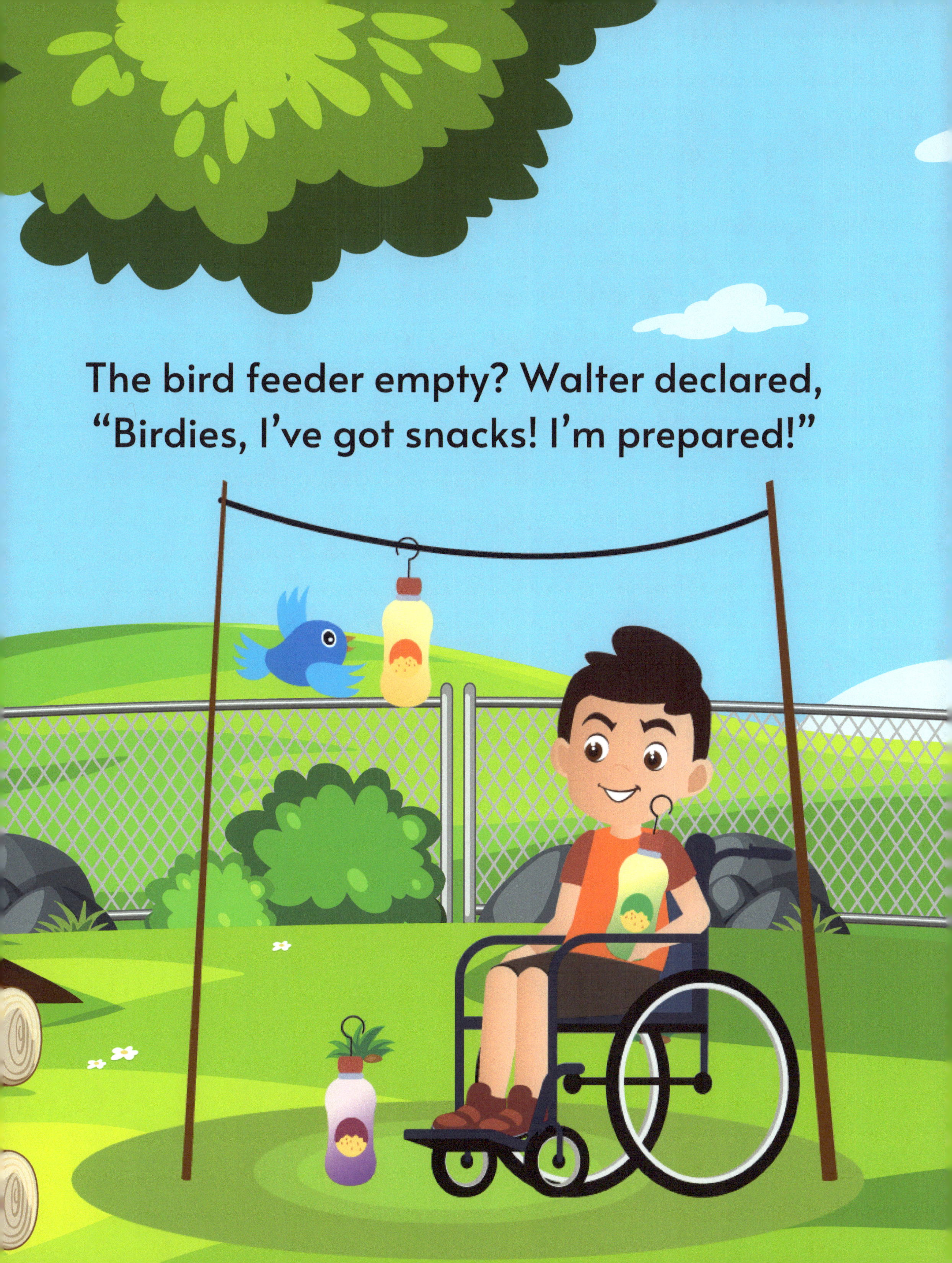

The bird feeder empty? Walter declared,
"Birdies, I've got snacks! I'm prepared!"

Walter tucked the sheets just right,
"Willow, this bed's ready for tonight!"

Their friends pitched in, with glee galore,
"You clean the windows, we'll sweep the floor!"

"Washing windows?
Let's see who'll dare!"

Chores aren't boring—they can be fun,
When everyone helps, the work gets done!

Laundry piled high—what a sight!
"Walter, don't mix my socks with white!"

Clothes on the line, blowing in the breeze,
Pete got tangled, "Help, I'm stuck in these!"

Willow grinned as she fed the cat,
"Stop purring so loud—you're getting too fat!"

"Trash bags are heavy!"
Walter groaned.
"Careful!" said Willow, "That one just moaned!"

Walter spun, "Next chore? No fears!" Willow laughed, "But let's rest our gears!"

Cooking dinner was a daring feat,
"Curry?" Great!
But don't burn the meat!"

"Hard work rocks!" Willow gave a shout,
"It's the best way to help out!"

Their work was done, the house looked great,
Mom peeked in, "I might just faint!"

"Let's earn our pay and
save it up—
Or buy some cotton candy
to fill our cup!"

Walter winked, "How about a treat?
A fizzy soda and something sweet?"

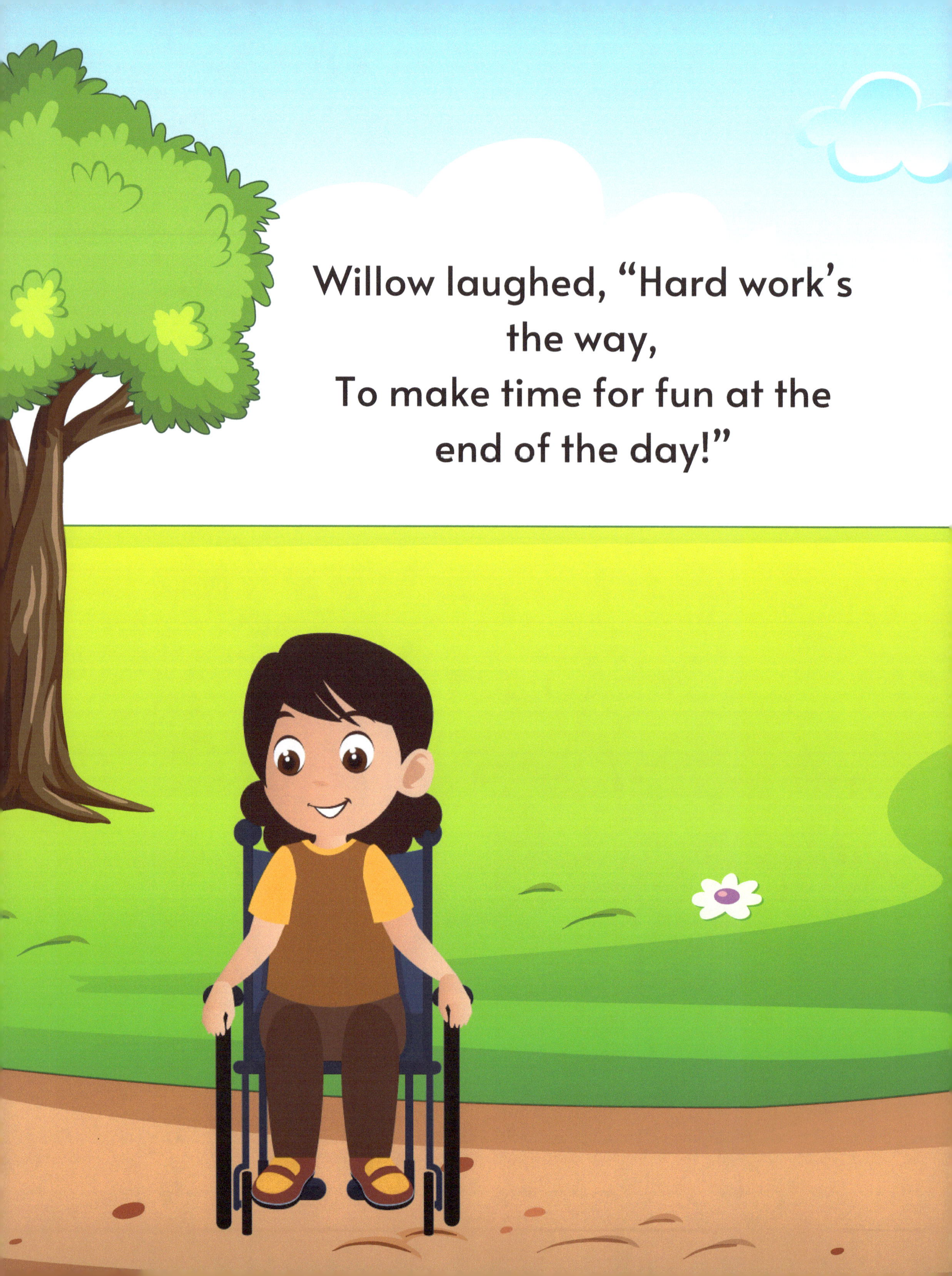

Willow laughed, "Hard work's the way,
To make time for fun at the end of the day!"

Helping at home can lighten
the load,
Even when you're on wheelie
mode

Mom and Dad grinned,
"What a team!
Our house is clean—it's like a dream!"

So grab a mop, a rag, or broom,
And clean your house from room to room!

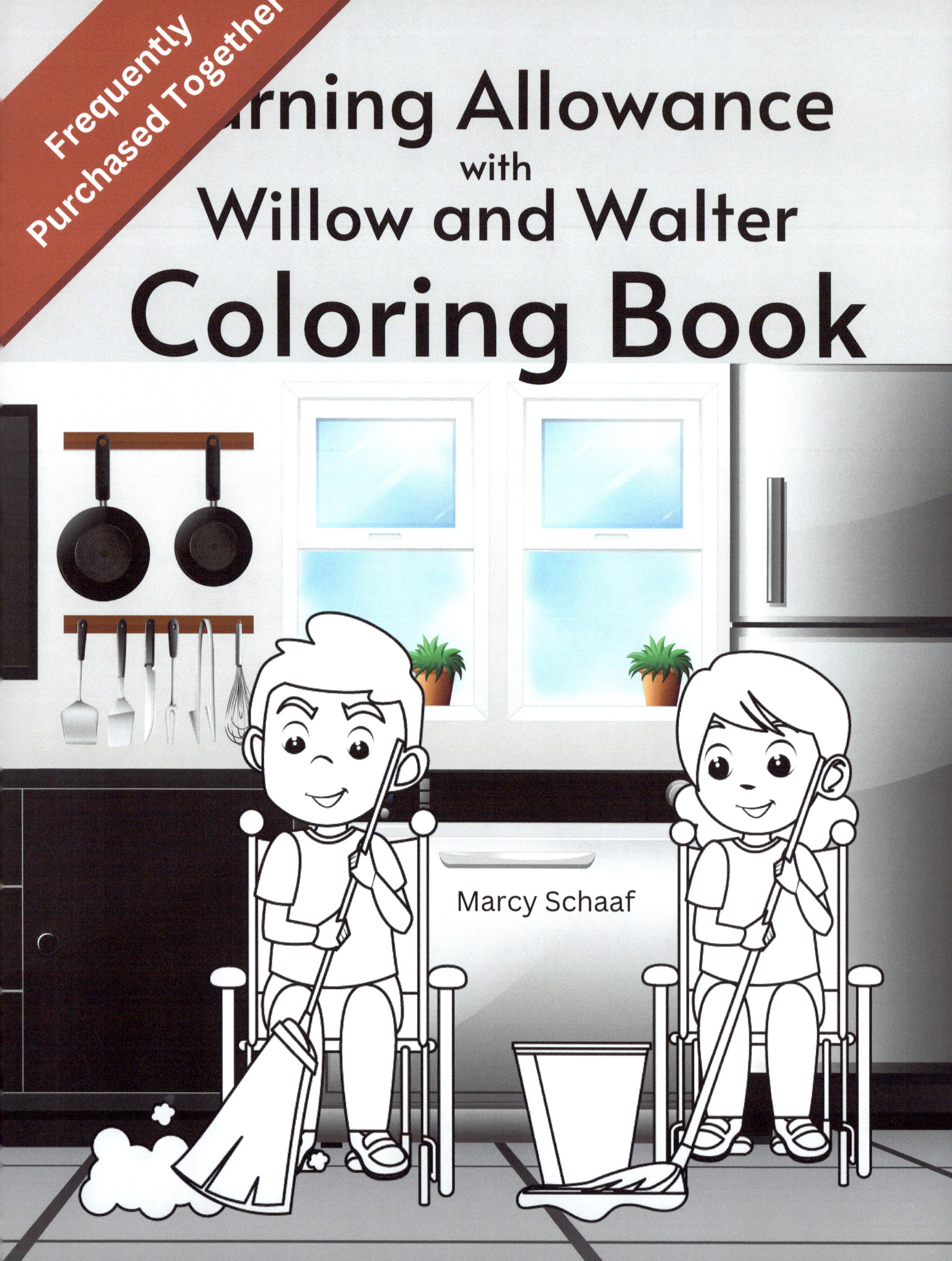

Frequently Purchased Together
arning Allowance
with
Willow and Walter
Coloring Book
Marcy Schaaf

Bonus FREE
Activity Guide

Activity Guide

"Earning Allowance with Willow and Walter"

1. Teamwork Chore Chart

Objective: Create a family chore chart inspired by Willow and Walter's story.

Materials Needed: Poster board or paper, markers, stickers, and a ruler.

Activity:

List chores from the book (e.g., sweeping, mopping, feeding pets) and any family-specific chores.

Assign tasks to each family member for the week.

Add a column for allowance earnings or rewards for completed tasks.

Decorate the chart with fun drawings or stickers.

2. Design Your Dream Allowance

Objective: Imagine how to spend or save an allowance creatively.

Materials Needed: Paper, crayons or colored pencils.

Activity:

Draw or write about what you'd buy or save up for if you earned an allowance.

Discuss the importance of saving vs. spending.

3. Chore Relay Race

Objective: Make chores fun with a timed family relay race.

Materials Needed: Brooms, dusters, laundry baskets, toy food or objects to mimic chores.

Activity:

Set up chore stations: sweeping, dusting, folding clothes, etc.

Time each participant completing the tasks.

Celebrate with small prizes or stickers for participation.

4. Chore Adventure Story

Objective: Write your own chore adventure inspired by Willow and Walter.

Materials Needed: Notebook, pens, or a computer.

Activity:

Imagine new challenges Willow and Walter might face while doing chores.

Write or draw your story, focusing on teamwork and fun.

5. Chore Reward Jar

Objective: Create a visual way to track chore rewards.

Materials Needed: Jar, slips of paper, markers, and stickers.

Activity:

Decorate the jar with stickers and write "Chore Rewards" on it.

Add slips of paper with small rewards (e.g., extra screen time, family movie night).

Each time a family member completes a chore, let them draw from the jar!

6. Role-Play Chore Day

Objective: Encourage empathy and understanding through role-playing.

Materials Needed: Household items for chores.

Activity:

Assign family members different roles (e.g., sweeping like Willow, mopping like Walter).

Act out the chores in a fun and silly way.

7. Discussion Time: Why Chores Matter

Objective: Reflect on the lessons from the story.

Materials Needed: None.

Activity:

Ask questions:

What was Willow and Walter's favorite chore?

How did they work together as a team?

Why is it important to help out at home?

Discuss how teamwork and chores can make life better for everyone.

Join Our Book of the Month Club!

Looking for the perfect gift that keeps on giving? Join our Book of the Month Club! For just $25 a month, or $250 if you purchase a year upfront, you or your loved ones will receive a handpicked children's book every month, straight to your doorstep.

Here's how it works:
Choose from 15 different languages to receive bilingual books that make learning fun.
Enjoy monthly shipments of our exclusive books that inspire, teach, and entertain children of all ages.
Each month's book is carefully selected to provide a new adventure, valuable lesson, and a chance to explore cultures from around the world.
It's the perfect gift for birthdays, holidays, or just because! Whether you're nurturing a young reader or encouraging language learning, our Book of the Month Club is designed to bring joy to every bookshelf.

Exclusive Bonus: As part of your membership, you'll also receive a monthly podcast about our featured book delivered straight to your email! Listen in for behind-the-scenes insights, fun facts, and tips for making storytime even more magical.

Sign up today at www.Booksbyschaaf.com and start enjoying the gift of reading all year long!

Books By Schaaf

www.BookBySchaaf.com

Song Some books have a song that can be downloaded from our website!

Podcast series about each books on TikTok.

Activity Guide companion's for each storybook can be found on our website.

Find us at:

www.ingramcontent.com/pod-product-compliance
Lightning Source LLC
Chambersburg PA
CBHW041626110726
48005CB00002B/516